You and I

Katherine MacLeod

BookLeaf Publishing

Presentation by *BookLeaf Publishing*

Web: www.bookleafpub.com

E-mail: info@bookleafpub.com

ISBN: 978-93-95784-03-0

First edition 2022

DEDICATION

For those with lonely minds too loud in the silence of the night

ACKNOWLEDGEMENT

First and foremost, to my family. You gave me life and then you continued to build it with me. I don't think I've ever said it, but thank you.
To Liv for being my support, editor and sounding board all in one

and Lottie for reading through all of my thoughts with no complains. The words on these pages wouldn't be what they are without the two of you.
To Gi - thank you for simply being my person.

PREFACE

I hope this collection of words can help bring you some of the peace it did me

My Almost Lover

We meet
Eyes catch
Smile shared
Nothing less, nothing more

- a kiss goodbye to my almost lover

Flowers

That day you bought me flowers
Not because you needed to
But because you wanted to
I didn't see the red of the roses
All I saw
Was "I love you"

You Never Said It

You never said it

But I saw it
In the early mornings
And through the late nights

And I heard it
In "I wish you were here"
And "I'll always be there"

And I felt it
God, I felt it
In your heat
And your hands
And your heart

You never said it
But I knew
(You loved me too)

For Us

We're not together
But we're not not together

There're no labels
Or expectations
Just feelings

It's not forever
But for now
It's for us

Only Time Will Tell

Your skin on mine
Lips to neck
Fingers intertwined

Is this heaven?
Or is this hell?

(Only time will tell)

Just Friends

We're just friends
But then you hold me
And you kiss me
And you touch me
And I forget
        We're just friends

Yours Now

You take up
So much of my heart
That I fear
It is more yours now
Than it ever was mine

3am

It’s 3 am
I can’t sleep
The sun isn’t up
Yet the moon is falling

The silence is heavy
Each sound deafens
My eyes stay closed
Hoping, trying
To steal just seconds more with you

You.

You.
Are all of my good days

You.
Are all of my bad days

You are my sad songs
And my happy nights
My best weeks
And loudest sighs

Love On My Lips

And I left

Love on my lips
Salt on my skin
Not because I didn't love you
But because I didn't know you

My Favourite Story

And we didn't get our happy ending
But it's still my favourite story

Forgetting You

You told me it would get better
And it did
You told me it would hurt less
And it does
You told me I would forget you
But I didn't

You're Not Here

I watch
        To see you
I breath
        To smell you
I listen
        To hear you
I sleep
        To touch you

- but you're not here

Reminders

And so each day I'm reminded
That maybe
We were meant to meet
But not meant to be
And I wonder
Why it hurts so much
When it lasted so little

Nothing I Want

There is nothing
I want more

There is nothing
I want less

Than you

I Find You

I find you
In my tears
In my cries
In my deepest fears
I will always find you
For you trapped me here

Left Unsaid

You and I
Ended before we began
And
Gosh,
We left so much unsaid

I Want To Be Yours

I can be anything I want to be in this world
Except for the one thing I want most

(I want to be yours)

Wrong Person

It hurts that I met you
Right time
Right place

Wrong person

Crossed Lines

The lines in our lives crossed
And for that one moment in time
I could touch you
And feel you.
My god,
Just imagine
What life could be
If instead of crossing our lives joined

Your Loss

I’ve learnt
To love myself
The way
I could have loved you

Your loss
Not mine

www.ingramcontent.com/pod-product-compliance
Lightning Source LLC
Chambersburg PA
CBHW051719130826
49812CB00034B/1253
9789395784030